W9-DFY-049

# Taking Aim
## How to *Accurately* Apply Scripture

*From the Bible-Teaching Ministry of*
**CHARLES R. SWINDOLL**

# Taking Aim: How to Accurately Apply Scripture

*From the Bible-Teaching Ministry of Charles R. Swindoll*

Charles R. Swindoll has devoted his life to the accurate, practical teaching and application of God's Word and His grace. A pastor at heart, Chuck has served as senior pastor to congregations in Texas, Massachusetts, and California. Since 1998, he has served as the founder and senior pastor-teacher of Stonebriar Community Church in Frisco, Texas, but Chuck's listening audience extends far beyond a local church body. As a leading program in Christian broadcasting since 1979, *Insight for Living* airs in major Christian radio markets around the world, reaching people groups in languages they can understand. Chuck's extensive writing ministry has also served the body of Christ worldwide and his leadership as president and now chancellor of Dallas Theological Seminary has helped prepare and equip a new generation for ministry. Chuck and Cynthia, his partner in life and ministry, have four grown children, ten grandchildren, and two great-grandchildren.

Published by IFL Publishing House, A Division of Insight for Living
Post Office Box 251007, Plano, Texas 75025-1007

**Editor in Chief:** Cynthia Swindoll, President, Insight for Living
**Executive Vice President:** Wayne Stiles, Th.M., D.Min., Dallas Theological Seminary
**Writers:** John Adair, Th.M., Ph.D., Dallas Theological Seminary
    Derrick G. Jeter, Th.M., Dallas Theological Seminary
**Content Editor:** Amy L. Snedaker, B.A., English, Rhodes College
**Copy Editors:** Jim Craft, M.A., English, Mississippi College
    Kathryn Merritt, M.A., English, Hardin-Simmons University
**Project Coordinator, Creative Ministries:** Noelle Caple, M.A., Christian Education, Dallas Theological Seminary
**Project Coordinator, Publishing:** Melissa Cleghorn, B.A., University of North Texas
**Proofreader:** Paula McCoy, B.A., English, Texas A&M University-Commerce
**Designer:** Kari Pratt, B.A., Commercial Art, Southwestern Oklahoma State University
**Production Artist:** Nancy Gustine, B.F.A., Advertising Art, University of North Texas

ISBN: 978-1-57972-971-4
Printed in the United States of America

# Table of Contents

# A Letter from Chuck

Life has many disappointments. Perhaps there is none greater than the realization that you have been biblically abused. By that I mean you have been the victim of someone who twisted Scripture, forcing it to mean something it does not mean . . . and then you believed this twisted version with all your heart, only to discover later that the information was fallacious or erroneous . . . that it was, in fact, dangerous to your spiritual health and growth.

I don't hear much about biblical abuse these days. Nevertheless, it's one of the major problems facing the church today. I think we could call biblical abuse the ultimate rip-off—it's the realization that the information you were given allegedly as truth from the Bible was, in fact, the result of the mishandling of Scripture and has since caused you to miss the target of accurate Bible application.

Understand, this has nothing to do with sincerity. Many people who mishandle the Word are very sincere. It really has little to do with theology. Some who have their theology straight can still mishandle Scripture. It has very little to do with being a "Christian celebrity." Famous, well-known personalities who draw large audiences can still mishandle Scripture. So let's put to bed, once and for all, the idea that a person's sincerity, expertise, or popularity will cover the problem of his or her mishandling Scripture. It's not true. We can all, at times, slip into the problem of misrepresenting God's Word.

The church—that means Christians like you and me—desperately needs people who carefully handle the Word of God, both personally on their own and in the teaching of Scripture. This lack of skilled Bible students is the real disease. Frankly, I don't think we ought to skirt it; we ought to address it. That's why this little book, *Taking Aim: How to Accurately Apply Scripture*, is so important.

Following a method popularized by my teacher, mentor, and friend, the late Dr. Howard Hendricks (or "Prof," as his former students like to call him), this volume will walk you through the basics of "taking aim," so that you can hit the target of accurate Bible application. The chapters in this book will present a method of Bible study in an accessible and easy-to-follow fashion. After the presentation of these steps to follow, we have included a workbook section that allows you to work through the method for yourself in different sections of Scripture.

Not only will the method help point you toward a more accurate handling of Scripture so you can avoid becoming a victim of biblical abuse, it will also make clear what should be the end result of all Bible study: application. Each of us, by taking aim through our reading and study of God's Word, will hit the target only by consistently applying it to our lives. Handling Scripture accurately without application leaves us with a heady faith that lacks heart. Allow this book to tie the whole process together for you, leading toward greater personal transformation and a spiritual impact that brings glory to God.

Charles R. Swindoll

# Orientation

*by Howard G. Hendricks*

Jeanne and I were vacationing on the West Coast several years ago with our son Bill. We had a friend there who owned a plane, and one day he asked if we wanted to fly with him to Santa Catalina Island. We accepted, and the next morning we were zooming down a runway heading up into the skies over Orange County.

After we leveled off over the Pacific, our friend turned to Bill, who was riding copilot, and shouted over the whine of the engine, "How'd you like to try your hand at flying?"

Always one for adventure, he replied, "Sure." Bill had never flown a plane in his life—but what difference did that make?

Our friend gave him some brief instruction in the art of flying—sort of a "crash course," you might say. Then he handed over the controls, and Bill was in command. Things went along uneventfully as long as we flew straight ahead. But after a couple of minutes the pilot shouted, "Why don't you try a turn."

Bill banked to the left, and suddenly I felt a bit dizzy. A moment later our friend said, "OK, try the other way," and the plane banked to the right. Now Jeanne and I both felt dizzy. We were quite relieved to see the pilot eventually rest his hand on the controls and level us off before taking over again.

"Not bad," he shouted to Bill, who was smiling like a Top Gun, "We only dropped about a thousand feet."

Obviously learning to fly takes a lot more than just handing the controls to someone and shouting, "Have fun." It requires skills that take years to develop fully. Apart from gaining that experience, you're taking your life in your hands.

The study of God's Word is no different. Learning to do it properly is a process that can't happen overnight. Yet that's exactly what we do with new believers when we tell them to get into the Scriptures, hand them a Bible, and expect them to take it from there. No wonder so many believers give up in frustration.

In this introduction, I want to give an overview of the Bible study process. First, I want to define what method in Bible study involves. Then I'm going to show the big picture of where the process leads and where you'll end up by following it.

## There's Method to the Madness

Let's begin with a definition. I define *method* in Bible study with three statements. First of all, *method is "methodicalness."* That is, it involves taking certain steps in a certain order to guarantee a certain result. Not just any steps, not just any order, not just any result.

The result governs everything. What is the product of methodical Bible study? What are you after? All along I've been saying that personal Bible study has a very specific aim—namely, life-change.

So, then, how will you get there? What process will lead to that result?

I propose a three-step approach that will guarantee life-change—three crucial steps carried out in a particular order.

 ## 1. Observation

In this step, you ask and answer the question, *What do I see?* The moment you come to the Scriptures you ask, What are the facts? You assume the role of a biblical detective, looking for clues. No detail is trivial. That leads to the second step.

 ## 2. Interpretation

Here you ask and answer the question, *What does it mean?* Your quest is for meaning. Unfortunately, too much Bible study begins with interpretation, and furthermore, it usually ends there. But . . . it does not begin there. Before you understand, you have to learn to see. Nor does it end there, because the third step is . . .

 ## 3. Application

Here you ask and answer the question, *How does it work?* not, Does it work? People say they're going to make the Bible "relevant." But if the Bible is not already relevant, nothing you or I do will help. The Bible is relevant because it is revealed. It's always a return to reality. And for those who read it and heed it, it changes their lives.

# It Takes Firsthand Knowledge

So method is methodicalness. But let me add a second statement to the definition: *Method is methodicalness, with a view to becoming receptive and reproductive.*

Do you want to make an impact on your society? First, the Scripture has to make an impact on you. It's the analogy of the sperm and the egg. Neither the male sperm nor the female egg is capable of reproduction. Only when the sperm impacts and is embraced by the egg is there conception and reproduction.

So it is in the spiritual realm. When God's Word and a receptive, obedient individual get together, watch out. That's a combination that can transform society. And that's what personal Bible study is designed to do — to transform your life and, as a result, transform your world.

A third statement completes our definition: *Method is methodicalness, with a view to becoming receptive and reproductive, by means of firsthand acquaintance with the Word.*

Once again, there's nothing to beat prolonged personal exposure to the Bible. It's vital. Without it, you'll never be directly involved with what God has to say. You'll always have to depend on an intermediary. Imagine dealing with your spouse on that basis. How long do you think your marriage would last? The same is true with God. There is no substitute for firsthand exposure to His Word. . . .

# Always Keep the Big Picture

So that is an overview of where we are going and how we're going to get there. Every time you come to a portion of God's Word, approach it in terms of the big picture:

Observation: What do I see?

Interpretation: What does it mean?

Application: How does it work?

That's the destination. Let's get started on the exciting journey.

# How to Use This Book

Welcome! We're so glad you've chosen to take aim at accurately applying the truth of Scripture to your life. This book is designed to help you do just that.

The chapters in the first section of this book present the three steps of Bible study: observation, interpretation, and application. Read these chapters carefully and take notes. Highlight those portions that you'll want to review. And by all means, make sure to read this book with an easy-to-read translation of the Bible at hand. You'll find numerous helpful examples that illustrate the various aspects of the three steps of Bible study.

The second section is interactive. It points you to four different passages from four different genres, or literary forms, of the Bible — narrative, poetry, prophecy, and epistle. These segments give you the opportunity to practice the Bible study method. For each workbook segment, you will read the designated Bible passage and then answer a variety of observation, interpretation, and application questions. Look closely at the kinds of questions asked, and view these segments as opportunities to observe the three-step method in practice. As you work through the passages, feel free to make additional observations, ask further interpretive questions, and make applications not indicated in our workbook segments.

One other note: as you get more serious about Bible study, you'll find yourself in need of resources that answer specific questions, resources such as a Bible dictionary, a Bible atlas, a reputable Bible commentary, and a concordance. We have included some recommendations on our Resources for Probing Further page near the back of this book. If you're on a limited budget, a good study Bible will include each of these elements in shorter form.

As with many things, you'll get out of your study what you put into it. So take aim and strive to hit the target of consistent Bible application, day in, day out.

# Taking Aim

## How to *Accurately* Apply Scripture

# Learning to Aim

*This section will help you learn the steps of observation, interpretation, and application. To make the most of these chapters, keep a Bible nearby and carefully think through each of the examples provided.*

# Step One

## Observation

Let's begin this chapter on observation with a quick bit of detective work. Imagine yourself a police officer taking a report from a distraught woman whose purse has been snatched. The culprit got away, but the woman mentions seeing a witness to the crime who has since disappeared. If found, this witness might enable you to locate the criminal and prevent him from snatching any other purses. Upon taking the report, you look back over the description of the witness.

> *Caucasian male. Six feet tall. Wearing a tweed, deerstalker hat. Seen with a tobacco pipe clenched between his teeth while looking through a magnifying glass at a nearby footprint.*

Of course, being one of the brightest officers on the force, you immediately think of the famous detective Sherlock Holmes. Even this brief description makes his identity obvious to the general reader.

More than a century after his creation, the name Sherlock Holmes has become synonymous with the word *detective*. A master of his craft, Holmes solved crimes that had left police scratching their heads in confusion. How did he do it? In a word: *observation.* Holmes observed the physical world, mastered its laws, and understood its workings. From this detailed knowledge, Holmes deduced the solution to crimes many thought unsolvable.

Another compelling, if lesser-known, fictional detective is one Father Brown, created by G. K. Chesterton as something of an antithesis to Holmes. Brown, too, was a master detective, observing the world around him, with a particularly keen understanding of humanity.

Both the private eye from 221B Baker Street and the parish priest from London uncovered the truth about criminal acts through their powers of observation. Whereas Holmes rose to the top of his profession because of his knowledge of the physical world, Brown served the world precisely because he understood the workings and motivations of human beings, morally and spiritually. Holmes relied on deduction. Brown relied on intuition. Both, however, observed. And both deduction and intuition are needed for effective observation in Bible reading.

Observation is an important element to solving a tangled mystery, and it is absolutely crucial for Bible reading, study, and application. What separates the great Bible readers from the rest of us is the same as what separates great detectives from the rest of the population: everyone sees, but the great ones *see well.* We all perceive certain things about our environments, but we cannot become keen observers of Scripture until we learn to see the right things. Those who see well have learned to use the reasoning of both Holmes and Brown, mixing deduction with intuition, balancing what is seen on the page with their knowledge of God and humanity. This comes first and most reliably through faith in the Savior, Jesus Christ.

Ultimately, improving our powers of observation involves focusing on both *how* we see and *what* we see. A better handle on these topics will lead us to become better Bible readers—and may even help solve the mysteries before us!

## How Do We Observe?

Before we delve into the nuts and bolts of observation, we need to ensure that we approach the text in the proper spirit and with the proper focus. We must follow four key principles.

First, to observe the Bible well, we must *be attentive*. Giving our undivided attention to a task is a great deal more difficult today than it was a hundred years ago. With more and more around us designed to capture our attention, we find ourselves focusing less on any one thing. The results? Our thoughts are divided. We glean less from the world around us. We see only the surface of things, without drilling down to their substance. When we come to the Bible, such a perspective simply is not an option for God's people. As believers, we want to know Him personally, to have a thriving and lively relationship with Him that drives us to live and act in accordance with His will. Fostering that kind of relationship requires attention to the details. When we think of those closest to us, we think of people concerned with the details of our lives, interested in the real substance of who we are. Anyone else stands a bit removed. Our relationship with God works on the same principle. As we seek to know Him through His written Word, our attention to the details of Scripture illustrates our desire to enter into real and substantial relationship with Him.

Second, to observe the Bible well, we must *be deliberate*. This principle highlights one of the ways that we can show our attentiveness to God's Word. By being deliberate in our approach to Scripture, we demonstrate a desire to get into the details of His Word. First and foremost, this means that when we read Scripture, we do so repeatedly. God's Word is not like that grocery store novel meant to be read once and then discarded. The Bible contains deep reservoirs of truth. It yields insights as we skim its surface, and those truths expand in significance as we probe its pages. Therefore, when preparing to really dig into a passage, make sure to plan time to read it several times over. As you read, the passage will become more familiar to you, allowing you to make connections and see elements of the passage that were not clear to you with a single read-through.

Being deliberate also requires coming to Scripture with a well-defined idea of what we are doing. Flipping open the Bible to some random page for each day's reading might introduce you to a section of Scripture with which you were not previously familiar, but the practice will not, by and large, lead you to dwell upon the deepest truths of Scripture. Instead, approach Scripture with a plan, such as reading a certain passage that day or studying a Bible book over a certain period of time. Of course, learning this process of observation, interpretation, and application will help to further solidify that plan, whatever you happen to be reading.

Third, to observe the Bible well, we must *be curious*. When you open the Bible, prepare to see something new, something you have not encountered before. A lifetime of Scripture study will not exhaust its insights, even for the most astute student or tenured scholar. No one has mastered the Bible. And yet, for those who have been exposed to it throughout childhood or for decades during adulthood, the Bible can start to seem stale. The danger of over-familiarity is one we must all grapple with as we progress in our faith.

One way to protect against such a danger is by embracing an attitude of curiosity when we approach Scripture. Curiosity carries with it the all-important quality of expectation. When we come to Scripture, we should expect to discover truths previously unknown to us. This involves recognizing that Scripture still has much to teach us, that it is filled with valuable wisdom for our everyday lives. Curiosity in our reading of Scripture allows us to see ourselves as open vessels, and as Scripture's truths flow into us, we'll benefit from our increased understanding of God.

Fourth, to observe the Bible well, we must *be humble*. Humility goes hand in hand with our recognition of Scripture's value. When we believe the Bible can teach us, we have recognized our own neediness. The apostle Peter exhorted God's people to "humble yourselves under the mighty hand of God, that He may exalt you at the proper time" (1 Peter 5:6). With a humbled attitude, we place ourselves under the power of God as He speaks to us through the text. In humility, we open ourselves to change, growth, and maturity.

And why can we grow? We grow and mature precisely because God shows us new truths and makes clear to our hearts and minds how we should live. The Psalms teach us that God "humbles Himself to behold / The things that are in heaven and in the earth" (Psalm 113:6). As God does, so should His people. When we walk in humility, we have the opportunity to see beyond our own perspective. When we are humble, we are teachable. We have the potential for maturity because of our openness to God's work in our lives.

Be attentive. Be deliberate. Be curious. Be humble. With these four strategies in mind, try your hand at the following observation exercise.

*Instructions: The names of fifteen of the sixty-six books of the Bible are hidden in this paragraph. Find them all in ten minutes.*

I once made some remarks about hidden books of the Bible. It was a lulu . . . kept some people actually looking so hard for the facts and studying for the revelation, they were in a jam, especially since the books were not capitalized. But the truth finally struck numbers of our readers. To others it was a real job. We want it to be a most fascinating few moments for you. Yes, there will be some really easy to spot. Others may require judges to determine. We must admit it usually takes a minute to find one, and there will be loud lamentations when you see how simple it is. One little lady says she brews coffee while she puzzles her brain.[1]

# What Do We Observe?

Now that we have reflected upon the way we should approach the text, we can turn our attention to the particulars, specifically: *what should we observe?* Observing well involves reading well. When we know how to go about looking (being attentive, deliberate, curious, and humble), we can better see what to look for. Therefore, we can begin to benefit from our reading in a way we never have before. So what should we look for? We can focus our vision on eight key categories: words and phrases, names and places, repetition, comparisons, contrasts, cause and effect, emphasis, and true to life. You'll want to keep pen and paper handy so you can begin a list of your observations. In the following step, you'll add and answer questions about them.

## Words and Phrases

Words and phrases are the building blocks of the Bible. Often we aren't fully committed to our reading. What do you do, for instance, when you come upon a word you don't know? Do you try to figure out the meaning from context? Do you look it up in the dictionary? Do you do nothing? For the sake of time and convenience, we often overlook those unfamiliar terms and just plow through the text, desiring to finish our task more than to enhance our understanding. As you read, observe those terms that you don't know . . . and write them down. As you interpret the passage, you'll get to dust off that dictionary and consider the meaning of the term within the context of its surrounding passages.

This will add a depth to your reading of Scripture with just a little extra effort on your part.

Beyond looking for those words you don't already know, observe those terms that strike you as interesting, significant, or unique. Focus especially on nouns and verbs, the basic terms of any sentence. And if you see interesting combinations of words, note those as well. The words you come up with should prompt questions for further investigation.

> *In Mark 2:1–13, we read about when Jesus was teaching to a packed house and eventually healed a paralytic. In the passage, we can see multiple words and phrases that will need further examination in the interpretation step. What does it mean that Jesus was "speaking the word to them" (2:2)? What was the roof built of that allowed for the four men to dig a hole in it (2:4)? Who were the scribes (2:6)? What did Jesus mean by "Son of Man" (2:10)? Observing—and then answering—these kinds of questions presents the opportunity for greater depth and understanding of the text.*

## Names and Places

While looking for key words and places, good Bible readers should also be scouring the passage for names of people and places. Every name and place should make it onto your list of observations. People and places bring context to passages of Scripture, linking them with events in the physical, everyday world of successes and struggles and desires. Noting those mentioned in any one particular text presents the opportunity to take what we know (or can discover about) that person or location and relate it to the events or ideas portrayed in the passage. Further, we get a sense of the surrounding geography from noting the places mentioned in the Scripture. In most cases, people and geography play a vital role in gaining an understanding of the text in question.

> In Mark 3:1–12, we read that Jesus entered a synagogue filled with Pharisees. When He healed a man with a withered hand, the "Pharisees" left and began to conspire "with the Herodians against Him" (3:6). Writing down the names of these two opposition groups helps readers begin the process of placing Jesus in the cultural, political, and religious context of His time. Further, when Jesus withdrew to the Sea of Galilee and a great multitude followed Him from Judea, Jerusalem, Idumea, beyond the Jordan River, and from the area of Tyre and Sidon (3:7–8), we begin to get a sense of the wide geographic range of people interested in Jesus. We'd want to list each of these locations. Once we look at a map, we can see that even this early in His ministry, Jesus drew a geographically diverse crowd from both inside and outside Israel-proper.

# Repetition

In addition to looking at the basic building blocks of the text, we should observe the notable ways that the words relate to one another. The simplest of those to observe is repetition—looking for the same word or phrase repeated within the same passage. You might also extend this to words or phrases that are repeated often within Scripture, though this latter strategy requires some familiarity with Scripture as a whole. Ultimately, the main thrust of this step involves finding repeated terms within a passage. Observing repetition in the Bible offers insight into the previous themes and significant concerns of a particular passage.

> *The author of Leviticus repeated the term* **holy** *seven times in 6:14–30. This offers the reader a sense of the position of the priests within the community of Israel. These men were to be separate, not only in their person but in the food they consumed. Similarly, Paul repeated the phrase* **share . . . joy** *twice in Philippians 2:17–18, a letter he wrote from prison. That he offered such sentiments during this dark time of his life illustrates the deep way in which his faith had penetrated his heart. Joy flowed from him even in dark days. But his request for the Philippians to share their joy shows the apostle's continuing need for good news from his friends. The repetition in this passage shows the absolute centrality of joy—both giving and receiving it.*

## Comparisons

One common strategy in biblical writing involves making comparisons to enhance or explain the meaning of an idea or the significance of a person. By drawing lines of connection between a symbol and an object or idea, the Bible enhances our understanding of that object or idea.

Comparison occurs in writing but also in everyday life. When watching a sporting event such as basketball, we can easily tell which players are on which teams by looking at their uniforms. Those players wearing the same uniform play on the same team. With this principle in mind, we approach biblical comparisons by seeking out those things in the text that are alike. This may take on a number of forms, such as *personification*: ascribing human characteristics to animals or objects, as in Isaiah 55:12 or Psalm 114; *hyperbole*: the conscious exaggeration by an author for a heightened effect, as in Deuteronomy 1:28 or John 21:25; or *anthropomorphism*: ascribing human characteristics to God, as in Exodus 6:6 or Psalm 19:1. Usually comparisons occur as *similes* — look for the words *like* or *as* — or *metaphors* — when an object or idea is used in place of another to show likeness.

> *The Bible makes comparisons constantly, and while they occur throughout Scripture, we find them most often in the poetic sections of Scripture such as Psalms, Proverbs, and Song of Solomon. For instance, David used a simile to describe his desire to flee his fears, crying out, "Oh, that I had wings like a dove! / I would fly away and be at rest" (Psalm 55:6). Solomon resorted to metaphors when speaking to his child, advising, "Say to wisdom, 'You are my sister'" (Proverbs 7:4). In this, we get a very clear sense that Solomon wanted his son to have a close relationship with wisdom at all times, just as he would have with a sibling.*

## Contrasts

The Bible also uses contrast to communicate ideas. One of the easiest ways to understand a concept is to make clear what it isn't. By showing the differences between two objects, people, or ideas, the Bible allows us to see more clearly the real essence of those things in view. To bring back the basketball analogy, we can tell one team from another by resorting to contrast—purple and gold uniforms look dramatically different from green and white uniforms. In an instant, we understand which players play with which team.

One of the easiest ways to spot a contrast is to look for the word *but.* Whenever you see it, look out for the differences between the two things surrounding it.

> *When the prophet Amos pronounced judgment on God's people, he told of a famine that would come upon the land: "Not a famine for bread or a thirst for water, / But rather for hearing the words of the* Lord*" (Amos 8:11). With the use of contrast, Amos made painfully clear the needs of the judged people. Food and water they had in abundance, but what they truly needed and desired was a word from God . . . and because of their actions, they would not find it.*

Writers also show contrast by using *irony*: the use of language to express a different meaning than the one stated for the purpose of ridicule or sarcasm, as in 1 Kings 18:27 or Job 12:2; or *paradox*: the statement of truth in what appears to be a contradiction of ideas, as in Matthew 13:12 or Mark 8:35.

## Cause and Effect

Many points that the Bible argues and many actions that the Bible portrays follow a structure of cause and effect. When reading a passage, it helps to be attentive to this relationship. The Bible has a great deal to say about promises, all of which function on the basis of cause and effect: because God made a promise, a blessing (or a curse) will come to pass. One set of words to look for in seeking out cause and effect is the "if . . . then" statement. For example, *if* you fail to eat your ice cream cone quickly enough, *then* it will melt and make a big mess. The cause is the failure to eat the ice cream in a timely fashion. The effects are melting and messes.

> *Exodus 19:5 contains a significant "if . . . then" statement that illustrates the cause-effect relationship. The Lord told the Israelite people gathered at Sinai, "If you will indeed obey My voice and keep My covenant, then you shall be My own possession among all the peoples." When the people obey God's commands (cause), He will make them His treasured possession (effect). An example of cause and effect without the "if . . . then" statement comes in the Psalms, where the one who delights in the law of the Lord "will be like a tree firmly planted by streams of water, / Which yields its fruit in its season (Psalm 1:3). The cause here is delighting in God's law, leading to the effect of being spiritually fruitful.*

## Emphasis

Another significant factor to observe when reading Scripture is what the writer is emphasizing. Sometimes we can perceive emphasis when the author expressly reveals his purpose for writing. At other times, we see what receives greatest emphasis based on what comes first or what comes last. Authors will often place the most significant point at the beginning or end of their argument or story in an effort to draw attention to it. One other common way to perceive emphasis is to take into account the amount of words an author devotes to one topic—extensive remarks indicate emphasis, while only a line or two means that topic isn't as important.

> *We can perceive a number of examples of emphasis throughout the Bible. In 1 John 5:13, the apostle stated his purpose for writing the letter, emphasizing it so we would not miss it: "These things I have written to you who believe in the name of the Son of God, so that you may know that you have eternal life." Therefore, when we read 1 John, it makes sense to read it all in light of this one emphasized truth.*

## True to Life

One of the dangers of a process like the one this book lays out is that it can become too mechanical. The rules and directions in this chapter and the two that follow should function like kindling does for a fire. The focus is ultimately not on following the rules but on the text of Scripture itself and how that text resonates in our own everyday lives (Psalm 119:105). Part of bringing God's Word to rest in our hearts involves observing those portions that touch our everyday lives. Often, Scripture works on us in mysterious ways, and therefore, it's important to note those times when it touches a nerve or speaks to a situation especially close to our hearts. The Holy Spirit often works through moments just like these to effect lasting change in our lives. Further, observing circumstances such as these brings God's Word closer to our own experience. It helps us see God's involvement in our daily lives, making clear for us just how significant it was that Jesus, the Son of God, took on human flesh on our behalf.

So take note of those elements of Scripture that ring true in your own experience. As you make these connections, you bring the Bible more deeply to bear on your life, making it ever more a part of your thinking and doing.

# Conclusion

Clear-eyed observation is the first step to grasping God's Word in a way that impacts our thoughts and deeds. In G. K. Chesterton's story *The Tremendous Adventures of Major Brown*, another of his detective creations, the character Rupert Grant notes,

> Facts point in all directions, it seems to me, like the thousands of twigs on a tree. It's only the life of the tree that has unity and goes up—only the green blood that springs, like a fountain, at the stars.[2]

Observation is a key step, but it cannot stand alone. With observation alone, we have little more than a collection of facts. How those facts are arranged to point us heavenward is a matter for interpretation.

# Step Two

## Interpretation

Singer/songwriter Harry Nilsson had a curious musical career. As a producer and recording artist, Nilsson's most unusual album—which was accompanied by a coloring book and was later made into a television special—was a story titled *The Point*.

*The Point* is about a round-headed lad named Oblio and his dog, Arrow, who live in a pointed land. Banished to the Pointless Forest, where all things are pointless, Oblio and Arrow meet the Pointless Man, who has a point in every direction. He points out: "A point in every direction is the same as no point at all." [1]

What's the point of this story, and how does it relate to interpreting the Bible? For any passage of Scripture, there is only one interpretation—one point. We might apply this one point in many ways, but we can't have more than one interpretation of any particular passage. In other words, to have an interpretation pointing in every direction, much like the words of the Pointless Man, is to have no interpretation at all.

Many in our postmodern culture believe we can interpret the Bible any way we'd like, forming our own private interpretations. But God's Word doesn't allow for this. Peter made this clear in his second epistle:

> But know this first of all, that no prophecy of
> Scripture is a matter of one's own interpretation,
> for no prophecy was ever made by an act of human
> will, but men moved by the Holy Spirit spoke from
> God. (2 Peter 1:20–21)

What did Peter mean by that? At first blush, it might sound as
though Peter thought people couldn't understand Scripture on their
own. But this is not what Peter was saying at all. Individual believers
who rely on the guidance of the Holy Spirit as they study *can* interpret
Scripture. What Peter meant, as indicated by verse 21, was that all
prophecy—all Scripture—finds its ultimate source in God. In other
words, no Scripture reflects merely the personal opinion or interpretation of the writer or reader of God's revealed Word.

The purpose, or point, of interpretation is to determine what God
said in Scripture in order to determine what God meant by what He
said. The meaning we are looking for in a particular passage is God's
intended meaning, not the meaning we wish to ascribe to that passage.
In this way, we must be careful never to confuse the voice of God (the
interpretation of Scripture) with the voice of the reader (the application
of Scripture).

Often the Bible tosses its golden nuggets on the ground, and all we
need do is pick them up. It doesn't take special insight or knowledge to

interpret Exodus 20:13–15, for example. Even in the original language of Hebrew the prohibitions against murder, adultery, and theft mean: don't murder, don't commit adultery, and don't steal. Most often, however, the Bible buries its treasures deeper in the soil of interpretation. And those willing to dig will unearth the Bible's treasures and thereby have those treasures buried deeply within their souls.

## A Bridge to Somewhere

If the goal of interpretation is to determine what God said in Scripture in order to determine what God meant by what He said, how do we do that? We build a bridge—a bridge of interpretation.

At least twenty-one centuries separate the biblical world—when the Word of God was recorded—and our world, where we interpret and apply it. This separation has created a great chasm between the original audience, who had a relatively easy time understanding what God meant, and the modern audience, who often has to work harder to understand what God means. We bridge this gap with a question: "What does this passage mean?" That's interpretation.

The bridge of interpretation is made up of four pillars and an expanse, illustrated like this:

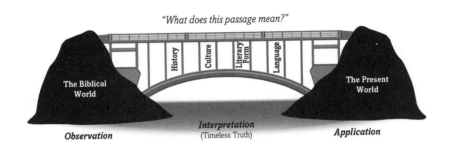

The bridge spans the gap between two points—the biblical world and the modern world. But the bridge consists of one span, not multiple spans—one theological interpretation, universal principle, or timeless truth per passage. Proper interpretation builds upon the specific discoveries found in the biblical text (observation) and distills them into one general principle (timeless truth) that can be specifically applied to a present-day audience (application). It is out of biblical observation and interpretation that we build biblical theology—or a belief system about God. It is out of biblical theology that we apply the truth of Scripture correctly and communicate it convincingly.

## Becoming a Biblical Bridge Builder

An old maxim warns us not to cross bridges until we come to them. This is a good idea when trying to cross a river. It's also good advice for those seeking to interpret Scripture. So, before we construct and cross the bridge of biblical interpretation, let's make sure we have all the qualifications we need to accomplish the task.

## Six Qualifications for Biblical Interpreters

In Acts 8, Luke recounted the story of Philip's encounter with an Ethiopian eunuch. On the road outside of Jerusalem leading to Gaza, Philip approached the Ethiopian's chariot and heard the man reading from the scroll of Isaiah. Philip asked the Ethiopian: "Do you understand what you are reading?" The man's response tells us something important about interpreting Scripture: "Well, how could I, unless someone guides me?" (Acts 8:30–31).

Biblical interpretation always begins with a biblical interpreter, someone who asks questions with the intent to discover God's mind as revealed in the Bible. And since "the mind of Christ" reveals the mind of God (1 Corinthians 2:16), the first qualification for biblical interpreters is *faith in Christ.*

In eternity past, God devised the plan of salvation through faith in the death and resurrection of Jesus, a plan "predestined before the ages" (2:7). The result of God's wise plan, worked out on Christ's cross and in the empty tomb, will bring the "mature" to their final "glory"—conformity into Christlikeness (2:6–7). If you'd like to discover how you might be saved through faith and gain this essential qualification, please read "How to Begin a Relationship with God," beginning on page 91.

The second qualification is to approach Scripture with *humility*. Just as we do in observation, when we interpret the Bible, we should be careful to keep our intellectual pride in check and approach Scripture with childlike humility. Jesus prayed, "I praise You, Father, Lord of heaven and earth, that You have hidden these things from the wise and intelligent and have revealed them to infants" (Matthew 11:25).

Third, we must be *willing to obey*. The writer to the Hebrews decried their immaturity and inability to hear more difficult teaching, though they had been believers for some time. These Jewish believers were babes sipping spiritual milk, though they should have been eating spiritual steak. What accounted for their spiritual malnourishment? They failed to put into practice even the elementary things they learned (Hebrews 5:11–14).

The fourth and fifth qualifications for the biblical interpreter go hand-in-hand. We must *pray* for the Spirit's illumination of a given text, and we must *work hard* to discover the meaning of the text. In Colossians, Paul prayed that the church would "be filled with the knowledge of [God's] will in all spiritual wisdom and understanding" (Colossians 1:9), and in his second letter to Timothy he admonished diligence in "accurately handling the word of truth" (2 Timothy 2:15).

The final qualification is a *dependence* on the Holy Spirit. Only the Spirit of God knows the mind of God. And the Spirit of God reveals the mind of God to those who possess the Spirit of God. Therefore, those who possess the Spirit of God possess the power to understand the mind of God (1 Corinthians 2:11–13).

## Two Assumptions to Be Accepted by Biblical Interpreters

Besides the six qualifications for biblical interpreters, there are two assumptions about the Bible all who wish to interpret it must accept.

First, the Bible is a work of literature. Each of the various books of the Bible was written by a specific person to specific readers in a specific historical, cultural, and geographical situation for a specific purpose. Each book was couched in the cultural setting at the time of writing, recorded in written language following normal, grammatical meanings. Each portion of a biblical book must also be accepted and understood in light of its larger context, taking into account the nature of specific literary forms and the principles of logic and communication.

Second, the Bible is a divine book. This makes the Bible unique among all other literature. It contains mystery, prophecy, parables, miracles, and doctrines. But because the Bible is the very revelation of God, it's also unified, though written over centuries of time by many different and diverse human penmen.

# Building an Interpretive Bridge

The construction of an interpretive bridge—the span between the biblical world and the present world that represents the timeless truth of a particular passage—requires four major pillars or supports. And though it isn't necessary to address them in the order presented, each one is important if we are to arrive at the proper interpretation of a given biblical text. For each of the items you wrote down in the observation step, you will want to ask and answer certain questions. Understanding the pillars will help you see what to ask and why it matters. This section will also help you become more aware of the many things you can include on your observation list.

## | *Pillar Number 1:* **History** |

History in the Bible concerns itself with three broad subjects: the history of God's activities in the world, the history of humanity, and the history of God's chosen ones—Israel and the church. Every interpretation of Scripture must take into account one or more of these subjects.

Regardless of the specific passage we've chosen to study, we must step back and ask questions about the book as a whole. Because every book of the Bible was written by a specific historical author to a specific historical audience living in a specific historical situation, to arrive at a general theological principle—a timeless truth—we must explore the specific history of each biblical book.

The two major sources used in re-creating accurate biblical history are the Bible itself (primary source) and extra-biblical references (secondary sources), such as histories about ancient Israel, Egypt, Babylon, or Greece, biographies about biblical personalities, a Bible dictionary, a Bible atlas, a Bible commentary, or a Bible encyclopedia. Looking internally at the Bible and externally at the work of Bible scholars, we want to determine the general historical setting of the author and the audience.

## Author

We must ask: *who is the author?* Often, the internal evidence in the Bible itself tells us the author's name, as with Paul's letters when he signed his name at the beginning. At other times, the author isn't specifically named, but because of stylistic patterns in writing (internal evidence) and long-standing written Christian tradition (external evidence), scholars can assign authorship to unsigned books, such as Moses to Genesis or Samuel to Judges. To find this out we first skim the book for signs of authorship. If we can't find clues to authorship internally, then we can turn to Insight for Living's two volume set of handbooks on the Old and New Testaments.

Once we feel confident about the author of a particular book, we need to investigate what we can discover about the author. At least ten factors help us paint a pen portrait of a biblical author:

| | |
|---|---|
| Ancestral background | Profession |
| Advantages in home or schooling | Influence on others |
| Relationships—marriages(s) and friendships | Faults, shortcomings, and sins |
| Character traits | Religious experiences |
| Habits and thought patterns | Spiritual and moral growth |

For some biblical writers, we are able to discover all or most of these details; for others, only a few.

## Audience

Once we have done some research to get a handle on the general historical background of a particular book of the Bible and a good picture of the book's author, we need to ask: *who is the audience?* Who were the folks that first received this particular letter or message? Were they Jews or Gentiles? Were they saved, unsaved, or apostates? And if they were believers, were they mature or immature in their faith? Where were they located—in Egypt, in Babylon, in Israel—and at what time? Why did the author address this audience? For example, the purpose of John's gospel was to convince his readers to "believe that Jesus is the Christ, the Son of God; and that believing [they] may have life in His name" (John 20:31). The purpose of Luke's gospel and his subsequent history in the book of Acts was to compile a careful account of Jesus's life and ministry and the ministry of the apostles (Luke 1:1–4; Acts 1:1–2).

## | *Pillar Number 2:* **Culture** |

While exploring the general historical situation, mark down particular references to the culture or customs. This is important because culture illuminates the specifics of God's Word, facilitates our understanding of God's Word, and illustrates the truth of God's Word.

Generally, when reading or studying Scripture, pay attention to what people think, say, do, and make. We'll want to write these down on your list of observations. Then we can consult biblical and external references to gain deeper insight. Specifically, look for these culture indicators and then ask questions like the ones below:

- *Political Positions/Systems:* The Bible speaks of kings and queens, governors, satraps, elders, Caesars, and tetrarchs. What was involved in these various political positions? We read that Nehemiah was a cupbearer (Nehemiah 1:11). But what did a cupbearer do?

- *Geography:* Why would one travel down to Jericho and travel up to Jerusalem? What's significant about the fact that when David fled from Saul he hid himself in the wilderness of Engedi (1 Samuel 23:29–24:1)?

- *Economics and Business:* What was the value of a shekel, a mite, a drachma, a talent, or a denarius? Why was business often conducted at the city gate (Ruth 4:1)?

- *Legal Systems:* The primary legal agreements mentioned in the Bible are covenants and birthrights. What were these and what made them important? Proverbs 22:28 warns against moving ancient boundaries. Why were these boundaries put in place?

- *Agriculture:* Why were vineyards often enclosed by a wall and watched over from a watchtower (Matthew 21:33)? What's spiritually significant about the concept of grafting (Romans 11:17–24)? Why were believers often called "lambs" or "sheep" (John 21:15–17)?

- *Architecture:* What is significant about the fact that David could walk on his roof in the cool of the night (2 Samuel 11:2), or that Daniel went to his roof chamber and prayed with the windows open (Daniel 6:10), or that the disciples met with Jesus for the Last Supper in an upper room (Mark 14:15)? Why were cities walled?

- *Military:* Who were centurions, and what were the size and importance of a cohort and a legion? What did Habakkuk mean when he wrote, "They laugh at every fortress / And heap up rubble to capture it" (1:10)?

- *Family Life:* What was involved in inheritance, marriage, and slavery in biblical times? What did Jesus mean when He said, "If anyone comes to Me, and does not hate his own father and mother . . . he cannot be My disciple" (Luke 14:26)?

- *Dietary Laws:* Why were Hebrews prohibited from eating a young goat boiled in its mother's milk (Deuteronomy 14:21)? Why were Jews allowed to eat certain foods but not others? What's important about Peter's vision of unclean animals in Acts 10:9–16?

- *Clothing:* Paul admonished women to cover their heads in church (1 Corinthians 11:5–10). What does that mean?

- *Social customs:* Why would Job tear his clothing and shave his head in mourning (Job 1:20)? Why would one mourn in sackcloth and ashes (Esther 4:3)? What did it mean to "heap burning coals on [an enemy's] head" (Romans 12:20)?

- *Religious Sects and Cults:* The Bible refers to the worship of the false gods—Baal, Dagon, and Molech. What were the practices of these religious cults? What was the purpose of and difference between the various Jewish sects—priests, Pharisees, Sadducees, scribes, and Herodians? Jesus accused the Pharisees of violating the command to honor father and mother because of the tradition of Corban (Mark 7:9–13). What was Corban, and what did it have to do with the fathers and mothers?

Once we understand the cultural impact during biblical times and derive a universal principle from biblical culture, then we can more accurately apply cultural concerns to our day.

## | *Pillar Number 3:* **Literary Form** |

In his *Reflections on the Psalms*, C. S. Lewis wrote: "The Bible, since it is after all literature, cannot properly be read except as literature; and the different parts of it as the different sorts of literature they are." [2]

While it recounts true, historical events, the Bible can be studied as if it were any other work of literature. Its books contain stories, poetry, parables, letters (epistles), and prophecy. And when it comes to interpretation, each unique type of literature requires a unique approach. Sometimes an entire Bible book can be classified under one type; other times several different types appear in the same book. That's why it's important to establish ahead of time what passage you will be studying.

## Narratives

For stories, or narratives, we want to focus on three items. First, we ask questions about the setting, noting physical, temporal, and cultural components. For example, we learn from the book of Jonah, Bible commentaries, and maps that sometime in the 760s BC—before Assyria sacked Israel (temporal setting)—God commissioned Jonah to leave his homeland of Israel and travel to the northeast, to the Assyrian capital of Nineveh (physical setting), which, ironically, was the cultic center of Ishtar and the worship of fish (cultural setting). However, Jonah fled from God to the southwest—the opposite direction—as far as modern-day Spain.

This establishes the *setting* of Jonah, but what can we learn about the *characters* in the story? This is the second item you want to note. How do the characters interact with one another? What do they say or think? And how do they act? In the book of Jonah, we discover that Jonah was a disobedient prophet of God, boarding a ship filled with salty sailors who pleaded to their gods when the seas grew violent. We also read that

Jonah confessed that God was the Lord of the sea, and Jonah told the sailors if they would throw him overboard the seas would become calm. What do these factors tell us about the attitudes, thoughts, and beliefs of the characters?

Finally, identify the nature of the *plot development*—the sequence of events that follow the model of beginning, middle, and end. When looking at your observations about the plot, ask and answer the following types of questions:

- What type of conflict is in view—physical (man against nature), character (either man against man or man against himself), or spiritual (either man against himself or man against God)?

- What makes the plot interesting or suspenseful—danger, tests, questions of destiny, or divine-human encounters?

- What are the relationships between the events—cause/effect, change/no change?

- What challenge(s) must the main character master—physical strength, resourcefulness, mental acuity, or spiritual strength?

- What changes occur between the beginning and the end of the narrative—solutions to problems or character growth?

- What do the details of the narrative tell us about the author's purpose—perspective on reality or teaching of morality?

As we consider narratives, we want to be on the lookout for a particular type of narrative called *parables*. Parables are unique and almost exclusively consigned to the New Testament. They are "short stories" that depict real life and, by way of analogy, are designed to teach specific spiritual truths, usually related to God's kingdom. Parables have four basic purposes: first, to reveal new truth to the believing person or people (revelational); second, to conceal truth from the unbelieving person or people (judgmental); third, to provoke a decision from the undecided person or people (persuasive); and fourth, to stir up the memory of the truth through the telling of concrete stories (perpetuative).

When it comes to interpreting parables, five guidelines apply:

1. Uncover the historical and cultural setting
2. Discover the problem being addressed in relation to God's kingdom
3. Uncover the central truth or its major points of comparison
4. Relate the details of the supporting scenery to the central truth
5. State the intended appeal or application

## Poetry

The Bible contains four basic styles of *poetry*:

| Brief and thematic lyrics | Pastoral love lyrics (Song of Solomon) |
|---|---|
| Descriptive and declarative praise and lament psalms (Lamentations) | Character depictions |

The distinguishing element of Hebrew poetry is the use of parallelism, the statement or restatement of previous lines or thoughts. Parallelism is a stereo-metric device, meaning similar ideas are repeated sometimes in the same words and sometimes in different words, driving home important ideas and aiding readers and listeners in memory. Five types of parallelism dominate biblical poetry.

1. Synonymous parallelism says the same thing but in different words (Psalm 2:1; 3:1).

2. Antithetical parallelism affirms the truth in the first line by offering a contrast in the second line (Psalm 1:6).

3. Climactic parallelism affirms the truth in the first line by exactly repeating it in the second line but adding a conclusion (Psalm 29:1).

4. Synthetic parallelism affirms the truth in the first line by repeating the thought in the second line and adding a conclusion (Psalm 14:2).

5. Emblematic parallelism presents a figure of speech in one line and explains it in another line (Psalm 42:1; 52:4).

## Epistles

The Epistles, or letters, of the New Testament are relatively easy to interpret because they follow logical progressions or arguments. Epistles usually open with a salutation, telling us something about the author and the audience and expressing a greeting. Introductions often include a report on the welfare of the writer and a blessing on the reader. Epistles follow a predictable pattern of construction: an introduction, an issue or problem needing attention, and a conclusion—in which the author gives a closing greeting, another wish for health, and a farewell salutation. Knowing the structure of the Epistles helps us get acquainted with the writer, audience, and central message.

## Prophecy

Prophecy, whether in the Old Testament or New Testament, basically either announces salvation or judgment. Prophetic salvation usually involves the future or end times when the Lord will rule and humanity will know peace. Prophetic judgment, however, is distinguished by these characteristics:

- The accused is given a summons.

- The specific accusation is given, usually because someone or a nation has violated the Law, often followed by a pronouncement of "woe."

- An announcement is made in regard to the accused that expresses either God's merciful intervention or just punishment.

The distinctive of prophecy is its visionary literature. Typically, prophecy is filled with symbolism—historical realities communicated through figures of speech instead of literal language. It involves the supernatural world of God, demons, and angels. Its scope is to transform the present state of things into a situation that can only be imagined in the future. The scenes portrayed in prophecy are cosmic, depicting strange characterizations of people, places, and events.

When it comes to interpreting prophecy passages, keep in mind these seven principles:

1. Interpret the self-contained prophecy unit first, and then relate it to the larger section of Scripture or book in which it is found.

2. Interpret biblical symbols by comparing them to symbols used by other writers of Scripture. For example, you should interpret Revelation in light of Daniel.

3. Don't forget: the basic purpose of prophecy is to either announce salvation or judgment.

4. Prophecy is primarily futuristic, using present images to reveal the unknowns of the future and especially about the "Day of the Lord"—that period of time in the future when God will judge His people and foreign nations, and will restore His people in perpetual peace.

5. Some biblical prophecy has already been fulfilled; some has not. Being familiar with the whole of prophetic literature prevents confusion concerning the prophetic past and prophetic future.

6. Implications of prophecy tend to be more cosmic and national, focusing more on the nation of Israel than on individuals.

7. Not every detail of extraordinary descriptions has interpretive significance.

## | *Pillar Number 4:* **Language** |

Once we've surveyed the historical, cultural, and literary backgrounds of a book or passage, we turn our attention to the meaning behind the words and phrases that make up that book or passage.

### Grammar

It's easy to get lost in the weeds when it comes to applying the interpretative process to grammar, especially when answering questions about etymology, or origins, of Hebrew and Greek words; about how a writer used particular words within the same book or in other books; or about how other writers used the same words. Applying interpretation to grammar is further complicated when wrestling with syntax—identifying parts of speech, types of sentences, and the function of key phrases—as well as understanding the grammatical structure of a passage.

The grammatical background, however, can be simplified by asking and answering: Is an assertion made, a command given, or a question asked in the main clause of a sentence? Are supporting clauses causal (expressing cause or reason), concessional (granting privilege), comparative, conditional, providing a purpose, or showing a result? How do these work together to convey meaning? For example, in John 3:16 Jesus makes an assertion that God loved the world, that He gave His Son, and that those who believe in the Son will never die. But in 3:17, Jesus expresses the reason that His assertion is true: because "God did not send the Son into the world to judge the world, but that the world might be saved through Him." These two truths together—the assertion in 3:16 and the reason in 3:17—give us confidence that our salvation is secure.

## Figures of Speech

As mentioned earlier, the Bible is made up of books that contain the same elements of any well-written work of literature, including figures of speech, such as simile, metaphor, personification, hyperbole, irony, paradox, and anthropomorphism. And just as in other literature, figures of speech are not to be taken literally. They are included to add color to the biblical narrative, to attract attention to important points, to make the abstract concrete, to aid in retention, to abbreviate ideas, and to encourage reflection.

When you encounter figures of speech on our list of observations from step one, ask not only the purpose but also the meaning of the word or phrase. Always use the literal sense unless there's good reason for using the figurative sense. Use the figurative sense when the writer states that the passage is figurative, if the expression fits into one of the classes of figurative language listed above, or if the literal sense fits into one or more of the following categories:

- it involves an impossibility
- it commands an immoral action
- it is contrary to the context and scope of the passage
- it is contrary to the general character and style of the book
- it is contrary to the plan and purpose of the author
- it involves a contradiction with a parallel passage of Scripture
- it involves a contradiction of established doctrine

# Crossing the Interpretive Bridge

Once we've answered questions of history, culture, literature, and language—the four pillars or struts holding up the interpretive bridge—we're just about ready to cross over from the biblical world into the present world of application. But before we make the journey, there's one more thing we need to do: we must summarize our interpretation into one simple, succinct, and clear statement. In other words, we need to identify and state the timeless truth taught in the passage.

## Timeless Truth

A timeless truth, as the name implies, is an abiding or universal principle that is not limited to a moment of time or a particular place. It is a general statement of truth that is applicable for all time and all peoples.

Sometimes the timeless truth is found lying on the surface of the page, as in "love your neighbor as yourself" (Leviticus 19:18) and "abstain from sexual immorality" (1 Thessalonians 4:3). At other times (most of the time), we must dig under the surface of the text.

*Genesis 11:1–9 tells of the Tower of Babel. God commanded both Adam and Noah to "fill the earth" (Genesis 1:28; 9:1). But human pride caused Noah's progeny to rebel against God and gather together in one place—on the plain of Shinar, where they built a city with a high tower. United by one language, the people joined together for security and social immortality. The Lord was displeased. He confused their language and caused them to scatter, thereby fulfilling His original command (11:9).*

*The timeless truth from this account would not be: "God is displeased with tall buildings" or "I should move away from my community," but rather, "Those who exalt themselves, God will bring low and judge."*

Now that we are standing on the span between the biblical world and our world—the timeless truth—we're ready to cross over to the other side and apply God's Word to our lives. So, let's not wait any longer. Let's cross over and learn how to make our study of the Bible personal and practical to our lives.

# Step Three

## Application

In 1637, a French philosopher named René Descartes first wrote what would become one of the most influential sayings in human history: "I think, therefore I am." Many of us have gone our entire lives without considering the meaning or the implications of this sentence, but every day we feel its impact on our culture. Regrettably, the thrust of this quote places an undue amount of focus on the mind. Descartes believed he could prove his own existence because he had thoughts. Deeds or actions simply did not factor into his equation.

If we mean to take seriously the call to Bible application, to use our observations and interpretations of Scripture to impact our day-to-day lives, then a mentality that focuses only on the mind—to the exclusion of our deeds—is a large problem. Both thoughts and deeds matter, and as we delve into what it means to apply Scripture to our lives, we shall find that true application works in both realms of our existence—the thoughts we think and the deeds we do.

## The Purpose of Application

For some, the practice of Bible study can become little more than an intellectual pursuit focused on the compiling and ordering of facts and events. Dutifully observing and interpreting Scripture, these students of

God's Word can fill a storehouse with details about God and the many ways He has made Himself known in history. However, the Bible calls us to a much higher pursuit than the accumulation of information. The Lord makes clear in His Word that He wants us to seek out spiritual growth and maturity. Ultimately, the goal of Bible study is not increased knowledge but a more focused and earnest pursuit of God's ideals for us in our day-to-day lives.

The writer to the Hebrews communicated eloquently on this subject. His readers had not matured as they should have, prompting him to chide and exhort them. He wrote,

> You have need again for someone to teach you the elementary principles of the oracles of God, and you have come to need milk and not solid food. For everyone who partakes only of milk is not accustomed to the word of righteousness, for he is an infant. But solid food is for the mature, who because of practice have their senses trained to discern good and evil. Therefore, leaving the elementary teaching about the Christ, let us press on to maturity. (Hebrews 5:12–6:1)

The contrast in this passage between the immature and the mature is striking. Drawing upon a "milk versus solid food" metaphor, the author made clear his readers' need for teaching and maturity. Most significant, though, is how he described their immaturity, noting that they were "not accustomed to the word of righteousness." In other words, the lack of maturity in these people was evident in their approach to life. We know they were not accustomed to receiving teaching about righteousness because they did not take that teaching and implement it in their lives, which would have led to increased maturity.

The spiritually mature, on the other hand, have worked at putting teaching about righteousness into practice. The result for these, according to the passage, was training in the discernment of good from evil. The immature often miss this difference, leaving them unable to walk in righteousness because they cannot find or separate it from wickedness. Maturity, then, is vital to living out our lives in the way God intends for us; it shows itself in our deeds, not just our thoughts.

Such a perspective is consistent with how God made human beings. When God created us, He did not create just a mind to think or just a body to act. Instead, He created a whole person whose thoughts and actions are to work in unison to fulfill God's design for His creation.

## Deeds

In the view of Scripture, we are what we do. Our practices and behavior distinguish us from one another. One man murders another. One man shows kindness to a stranger. These acts reflect something of an individual's identity. Scripture often characterizes people by their deeds. Psalm 1:6 teaches that,

> The LORD knows the way of the righteous,
> But the way of the wicked will perish.

The reference to *righteous* and *wicked* here points primarily to a state of being that is evident to anyone looking on. The emphasis is placed in the case of both the righteous and the wicked on their "way"—focusing on what they do.

It should be no surprise then when Paul—a faithful Jew who knew Scripture well—addressed his Roman readers regarding application of God's Word. He first called them to "present [their] bodies a living and holy sacrifice, acceptable to God, which is [their] spiritual service of worship" (Romans 12:1). By using the term *bodies* in this context, Paul showed he understood the biblical emphasis on deeds. The person who lives in right relationship with God is the person who understands the importance of acting in righteousness and of sacrificing personal desires for the sake of God's desires and direction.

## Thoughts

Human beings are also rational creatures. We don't just act. We also think, reflect, and process events and ideas in ways that fundamentally distinguish us from any other created being. And as a result of that reality, God cares not just for our bodies but for our minds as well. Continuing his exhortation to the church at Rome, Paul encouraged the believers there not to "be conformed to this world, but be transformed by the renewing of your mind, so that you may prove what the will of God is, that which is good and acceptable and perfect" (Romans 12:2). The apostle was not content to simply have the people offer their deeds without also seeking transformation of their minds.

Such an approach would lead believers right back into the problem that plagued the Israelites throughout their history—they offered sacrifices to God but without the changed heart to go along with those worshipful deeds (Isaiah 1:10–17). The hypocrisy of the people led to judgment from God and eventually exile from the land He had promised to their forefathers.

Living a life of deeds without a changed heart is not the goal for believers. Spiritual maturity—and thus true application—demands an emphasis on both words and deeds.

## The Principles of Application

When we think about actually applying the Bible to our lives, we consider a process that demands individual attention. Application requires each of us to think about our own situations and needs. Every believer finds himself or herself in different places with different struggles and pursuits. In one sense, then, application is intensely personal.

However, once observation and interpretation have been completed, there are five questions that anyone applying Scripture should answer. Not every question will work for every passage, but the questions, as a group, should provide a solid foundation to begin applying Scripture. With the results of your interpretation in mind, answer the following questions.

## Questions to Answer

*Is there a sin to confess?*

Many passages in Scripture will raise the issue of sin—both directly and indirectly. The apostle Paul is famous for his lists of behaviors to avoid. For example, Galatians 5:19–21 includes a list of clear deeds that characterize those who shall not inherit the kingdom of God. However, in many other passages, the sin to confess is a bit beneath the surface. Whichever the case, regular reading and study of Scripture will help each of us better distinguish the path between sin and righteousness.

*Is there an error to correct?*

Scripture is largely concerned with how we live our daily lives in terms of our deeds, but it also communicates clearly about the kinds of thoughts we should have about God and His world. As our study of Scripture challenges us, it will inevitably raise questions about some of our beliefs. A reading of the prophetic books may convince us of God's concern for the poor and needy in a way we had not seen before. Or a reading of Ephesians might show us the absolute necessity of God's grace for salvation. As we read, we must keep our minds open and malleable to correction.

*Is there a command to carry out?*

This is probably the easiest of all applications to identify. When Scripture makes demands on God's people—and it often does—we must be prepared to recognize the authority of God's Word and pursue a path of obedience. When we read Jesus's command, "Do not fear" (Matthew 10:31), we are then responsible to implement that reality in our lives. With the command before us, our next step — obedience — is not difficult to determine, even if it is sometimes difficult to carry out.

*Is there an example that challenges?*

Throughout Scripture we find good examples for living. Human beings almost implicitly follow the examples of those who surround them. Therefore, if we make a habit of surrounding ourselves with the stories and people of Scripture, we shall find our lives filled with good examples of faithful people — and bad examples of unfaithful people — to guide our steps in the direction God would have us go.

*Is there a promise to claim?*

When a Bible makes a promise, it might be to all people throughout history (Genesis 9:9–13), or it might apply to a narrower group of people (2 Chronicles 7:14). Hopefully through observation and interpretation, we can clearly determine the recipients of the promise. And if the specific contents of the promise apply to us today, we can continue to benefit from it as grounding for our hope in God and His specific plans for humanity and the world.

*Is there a prayer to pray?*

Lastly, we must keep our eyes open for prayers. In many cases — most notably the Psalms or the Lord's Prayer — the Bible contains specific prayers that we can transfer wholly to our context today. David's prayer of confession in Psalm 51 is no less powerful and meaningful today than it was three thousand years ago when he first penned it. Make a habit of incorporating the prayers of Scripture into your own prayer time with the Lord.

## Principles to Develop

Once you've asked and answered the six questions above, you are ready to develop an application principle. It should be general enough to apply to many people yet specific enough to involve real and concrete action. This passage will draw upon the insights of the previous six questions and combine those with the timeless truth you developed in your interpretation step. Bringing these insights together will yield one or more principles of application that pose particular actions for you.

Part of this process requires understanding when to draw principles versus when to obey specific commands. When Jesus told the disciples to go and untie a donkey (Matthew 21:2–3), the application for all believers is not to go loose all the donkeys that have been tied up. Rather, we understand from it the importance of obeying the command of Jesus. In contrast, when Jesus told His disciples to make disciples in every nation (28:18–20), we understand that to be a direct command not just for the disciples but for the church as a whole today. All of us should play some part in the making of disciples.

Whether the application has to be generalized from the text or corresponds quite closely with it, application requires drawing out a principle from the passage so that we can follow it up with action.

Creating application principles requires taking the truth discerned in the interpretation step, asking the appropriate application questions, and then stating the application principle. If the truth we discern from Psalm 119:105–111 is, "God's Word directs us through life's ups and downs," then we have to ask ourselves the six application questions above based on that truth. One may approach that truth and see a sin to confess for he hasn't allowed God's Word to direct his steps. Another may approach and see a promise to claim, that God's Word will indeed lead her through a difficult time. Others might see more than one application, combining insights from multiple questions. In the end, application is an intensely personal pursuit, and we must bring the truth of Scripture to bear on our own, individual experiences.

## The Practice of Application

Once we have understood the purpose for application—spiritual maturity—and the principles of application—asking questions to develop values to live by—we can move to the final consideration of application: just doing it. When we have a principle in hand and are ready to apply it, we will accomplish our goal by going through the following three steps.

First, *resolve to act*. No application takes place without a decision to implement it into our lives. Oftentimes, this comes as an instantaneous affirmation on our part. When reading and studying Scripture reveals a truth or practice that believers should embrace, many of us will decide to implement that practice right away. However, occasionally we run up against one of those difficult truths, a slayer of our sacred cows. These truths lead us to wrestle with what God's Word says to be true and right versus our own personal preferences or standard practices. Whether it is instantaneous or after a period of struggle, we must all make a decision to act upon God's revealed Word.

Second, *tailor a plan*. Many times when we decide to apply Scripture, we do so without thinking about how we will make that decision a reality in our lives. This can lead to inaction due to uncertainty. For instance, when you decide to forgive someone who has wronged you, the decision portion of that act is often the easiest. Then comes the question of how you will interact with that individual from then on. Will you go back to your old way of interacting before the breach occurred in the relationship? Will you address the issue of forgiveness with the individual? Questions such as these require some thought and planning; it's one thing to speak words of forgiveness and another thing entirely to live out the forgiveness on a daily basis. A plan is essential.

Finally, *follow through*. Both deciding and planning are individual pursuits, while applying the principles of Scripture involves a life well lived among others. The great commandment of Jesus, to love God with all our heart, mind, and strength, is followed by another, that we love our neighbor as ourselves (Matthew 22:37–39). The real significance of application lies at the heart of this command. We express our love for God in our love for other human beings—men and women, rich and poor, Christian and Muslim. Wherever there are people, there should also be Christians there to love them. And the only way that happens? By applying the Bible.

# Practicing Your Aim

*This section will allow you to practice the steps of observation, interpretation, and application. Using extrabiblical resources will enhance and deepen your study, but you can also answer the questions using only your Bible. Regardless of your experience or skill level, you can dive right in!*

# Narrative

*Genesis 39:6–12*

 **Observation**

Read the passage above and write down your own list of observations that fall into the eight key categories: words and phrases, names and places, repetition, comparisons, contrasts, cause and effect, emphasis, and true to life.

_____

_____

_____

_____

_____

_____

Now, answer a few specific questions as we guide you through the observation process.

How did Moses, the author of Genesis, describe Joseph in Genesis 39:6?

_____

_____

_____

What did the "master's wife," Mrs. Potiphar, do and say in verse 7?

_____

_____

_____

How did Joseph respond to Mrs. Potiphar in verses 8–9?

_____

_____

_____

How many times did Mrs. Potiphar speak with Joseph, and how often did he refuse her, according to verse 10?

_____

_____

_____

Where did Joseph go in verse 11, and who was with him?

_____

_____

What did Mrs. Potiphar do in verse 12, and what was Joseph's reaction?

_____

_____

_____

 **Interpretation**

Joseph was the slave of Potiphar, "the captain of the bodyguard"—or the head of Pharoah's security detail (Genesis 39:1). What is significant about this fact in relation to Mrs. Potiphar's sexual advances toward Joseph?

_____

_____

_____

_____

If Joseph had given in to Mrs. Potiphar's advances, it makes sense that he would have committed evil against his master because he would have violated Potiphar's trust. But in what way would it have been a "sin against God" (39:9)?

_____

_____

_____

What does the fact that Mrs. Potiphar spoke to Joseph daily (39:10) and then caught him (39:12) tell you about the nature of sin?

_____

_____

_____

What does the fact that Joseph tried to reason with Mrs. Potiphar (Genesis 39:8–9) and then had to flee (39:12) tell you about how we should deal with sexual temptation?

_____

_____

_____

Based on your observations and interpretation, what is the timeless truth in this passage?

_____

_____

_____

_____

 **Application**

Consider the timeless truth you wrote above. Ask yourself the following questions, and place a checkmark next to those that apply.

| Is there . . . | |
|---|---|
| a sin to confess? | |
| an error to correct? | |
| a command to carry out? | |
| an example that challenges? | |
| a promise to claim? | |
| a prayer to pray? | |

Before deriving your personal application principle, answer a few specific application questions to get you thinking about the practical implications of this passage.

Under what circumstances are you most vulnerable to sexual temptations (for example, when you're lonely, depressed, sick, tired, or even when you're successful or happy)?

_____

_____

_____

_____

What types of persuasion (words, sounds, sights, thoughts, or touch) are most likely to tempt you into sexual sin?

_____

_____

_____

_____

What is your game plan to avoid sexual temptation when the combination of circumstances and persuasion coincide in your life?

_____

_____

_____

_____

What personal application principle can you derive from your insights?

_____

_____

_____

_____

_____

_____

# Poetry

*Psalm 12:1–8*

 **Observation**

Read the passage above and write down your own list of observations that fall into the eight key categories: words and phrases, names and places, repetition, comparisons, contrasts, cause and effect, emphasis, and true to life.

_____

_____

_____

_____

_____

Now, answer a few specific questions as we guide you through the observation process.

Answer this question using only one word: What did David request from God in Psalm 12:1?

_____

What missing element of society was especially distressing to David?

_____

_____

What qualities characterize those who opposed David?

_____

_____

_____

How did David want God to help him, based on verses 3–4?

_____

_____

What did David expect God would do, according to verse 5?

_____

_____

What on earth, according to verse 5, would motivate God to act in such a way?

_____

_____

What characteristics of God, according to verses 6 and 7, would motivate Him to come to David's aid?

_____

_____

What reality did David affirm to conclude the psalm?

_____

_____

 **Interpretation**

In the Interpretation chapter, beginning on page 21, we discussed the five kinds of parallelism in poetry (synonymous, antithetical, climactic, synthetic, and emblematic). Which type is used in verses 1 and 8? How does the awareness of this particular parallelism help you understand what David was trying to communicate at the beginning and end of this psalm?

_____

_____

_____

_____

_____

How does the question the ungodly ask in verse 1 contrast with God's statement in verse 5?

_____

_____

_____

What does that contrast communicate about God's relationship to the wicked?

_____

_____

On what specifically did David base his faith that God would bring David into safety (see verse 6)?

_____

_____

_____

Based on your observations and interpretation, what is the timeless truth in this passage?

_____

_____

_____

 **Application**

Consider the timeless truth you wrote above. Ask yourself the following questions, and place a checkmark next to those that apply.

| Is there . . . | |
| --- | --- |
| a sin to confess? | |
| an error to correct? | |
| a command to carry out? | |
| an example that challenges? | |
| a promise to claim? | |
| a prayer to pray? | |

Before deriving your personal application principle, answer a few specific application questions to get you thinking about the practical implications of this passage.

Who do you identify with in the psalm—David or those who opposed him? Do you need to confess to any of the negative deeds David detailed in this psalm?

_____

_____


How can David's approach to the wicked inform your own dealings with people who do you wrong?

_____

_____

_____

_____


Do you have an expectation that God is going to remove wickedness prior to Jesus's return? How does this psalm inform your view on this question, and how should you order your life in light of that truth?

_____

_____

_____

_____

_____

What personal application principle can you derive from your insights?

_____

_____

_____

_____

_____

_____

# Prophecy

*Amos 5:1–7*

 **Observation**

Read the passage above and write down your own list of observations that fall into the eight key categories: words and phrases, names and places, repetition, comparisons, contrasts, cause and effect, emphasis, and true to life.

_____

_____

_____

_____

_____

Now, answer a few specific questions as we guide you through the observation process.

To gain a little cultural context from within the book of Amos, scan the book looking for the types of sins in which the people were engaged and write them below. If you need some direction, read Amos 2:6–8; 3:10; and 4:1.

_____

_____

_____

How did Amos describe the message he delivered to Israel in Amos 5:1–7?

_____

Which two images describe the people of Israel in verses 2 and 3?

_____

_____

What did God command the people to do in verse 4? If they followed His command, what would result?

_____

_____

_____

_____

Read the following verses, and describe the significance of each of the places mentioned in verse 5. (You can locate additional verses that refer to place names using a Bible concordance, while a Bible atlas can give you a sense of their location.)

Bethel (1 Kings 12:28–29)

_____

_____

Gilgal (1 Samuel 11:14–15)

_____

_____

Beersheba (Genesis 21:31–33; 46:1–3)

_____

_____

What one idea is repeated in Amos 5:1–7, mentioned twice by Amos?

_____

_____

_____

_____

What will happen to those who do not respect justice or pursue righteousness?

_____

_____

_____

_____

## Interpretation

An introduction to the book of Amos in a commentary would direct you to the historical context in the following question: Second Kings 14:23–29 recounts the successful—albeit, evil—reign of Jeroboam II, with a gain in territory that would certainly yield increased security and financial benefits. How would Amos 5:3 have sounded to Israelites following the leadership of Jeroboam II?

_____

_____

_____

Based on your observations in the previous section, what is the common historical significance of the three places mentioned in verse 5?

_____

_____

_____

Why do you think the people would have had the impulse to visit those places with judgment bearing down upon them?

_____

_____

_____

_____

What is wormwood? If you don't know, take the time now to look up the word in a dictionary.

_____

_____

_____

What will result for the people if they do not change their ways?

_____

_____

_____

Based on your observations and interpretation, what is the timeless truth in this passage?

_____

_____

_____

_____

 **Application**

Consider the timeless truth you wrote above. Ask yourself the following questions, and place a checkmark next to those that apply.

| Is there . . . | |
|---|---|
| a sin to confess? | |
| an error to correct? | |
| a command to carry out? | |
| an example that challenges? | |
| a promise to claim? | |
| a prayer to pray? | |

Before deriving your personal application principle, answer a few specific application questions to get you thinking about the practical implications of this passage.

God offered a command to the people back then (Amos 5:4, 6). In what kinds of concrete ways are you not actively seeking God?

_____

_____

_____

Are there aspects of your thinking that you need to change regarding these areas? Are there any passages of Scripture that can guide you in this regard?

_____

_____

_____

_____

_____

What steps can you take to build more "life-affirming" habits, rather than those associated with judgment and destruction?

_____

_____

_____

What personal application principle can you derive from your insights?

_____

_____

_____

_____

_____

_____

# Epistle

*Hebrews 12:1–8*

 **Observation**

Read the passage above and write down your own list of observations that fall into the eight key categories: words and phrases, names and places, repetition, comparisons, contrasts, cause and effect, emphasis, and true to life.

_____

_____

_____

_____

_____

_____

What is the first word the writer of Hebrews used to begin this section? To what does it refer?

_____

_____

_____

_____

The writer of Hebrews gave a number of imperative statements, or commands, in verses 1–3. What are they?

_____

_____

_____

_____

What primary metaphor did the writer of Hebrews employ in verses 1–2?

_____

_____

_____

_____

What words did the writer of Hebrews use to describe Christ?

_____

_____

_____

_____

What metaphor did the writer of Hebrews employ in verses 4–8?

_____

_____

_____

# Interpretation

What is significant to the Christian life about the race metaphor in verses 1–3?

_____

_____

_____

_____

_____

What is significant to the Christian life about the discipline metaphor in verses 4–8?

_____

_____

_____

_____

_____

How do these two metaphors work together?

_____

_____

_____

The writer to the Hebrews contrasted Jesus's struggle with sin and our struggle with sin. What does the writer say about these two different struggles, and how does that fit within his overall argument in the passage?

_____

_____

_____

_____

_____

_____

Based on your observations and interpretation, what is the timeless truth in this passage?

_____

_____

_____

_____

_____

 **Application**

Consider the timeless truth you wrote above. Ask yourself the following questions, and place a checkmark next to those that apply.

| Is there . . . | |
|---|---|
| a sin to confess? | |
| an error to correct? | |
| a command to carry out? | |
| an example that challenges? | |
| a promise to claim? | |
| a prayer to pray? | |

What encumbering sin do you need to lay aside? How can you go about doing that?

_____

_____

_____

How do you personally "fix your eyes on Jesus"?

_____

_____

_____

_____

_____

What discipline have you undergone from the Lord in the past? How did/does that discipline encourage you as a child of God?

_____

_____

_____

_____

_____

What personal application principle can you derive from your insights?

_____

_____

_____

_____

_____

_____

# Appendix

85

# Inspiration

*by Charles R. Swindoll*

One of the most strategic attacks the adversary wages against God's people has to do with the inspiration of Scripture. It continues to be *the* watershed issue of every new generation. The same tactic the serpent used against Eve in the Garden of Eden is the method he employs today with believers (Genesis 3:1–5; 2 Corinthians 11:3). If Satan can get us to doubt the truth of God's Word, then we have no standard by which to live, no clear message of salvation, no hope for the future, and no guidelines for the oversight and advancement of Christ's church. If the truth of the Bible is muddled or cloudy in our minds, we have nothing to guide us but our own opinions . . . and they are not enough! As my mentor Howie Hendricks often said, "A mist in the pulpit puts a fog in the pew."

As we study the Bible on our own, putting into practice the methods of observation, interpretation, and application, keep in mind that the foundation we stand on is *the inspired Word of God.* Paul revealed to Timothy this marvelous fact:

> All Scripture is inspired by God. (2 Timothy 3:16)

This may be familiar territory for you. But believe me, the words *inspired by God* sound eccentric to postmodern ears. Most people have never been taught about the inspiration of Scripture, and many who have been exposed to the biblical doctrine also have been instructed to question it, to disbelieve it.

However, if the Bible is not inspired, then it is not authoritative. And if it is not authoritative, then its commands are mere suggestions on par with every other book of morals. Furthermore, what it says about God is only as valid as any other religion's so-called holy writings. See the problem? With no inspired text, our guide becomes our feelings. It's the same slick lie Satan whispered in Eve's ear in the garden. Stop and think. That deception destroyed the spiritual lives of the whole human race.

The adversary will try everything possible to persuade us to doubt God's Word. Science, philosophy, psychology, and sometimes even shades of theology will be held out as proof that "people no longer accept the Bible as inspired." But they do. Jesus did. So did Paul. Many of us still do.

While there are numerous objective facts that support, and some would even argue prove, that the Bible is inspired, in the end we each find ourselves kneeling and trusting the wisdom of our infinite God over the limitations of human intellect. Without apology, without embarrassment, and without committing intellectual suicide, we believe by faith that God's Word is what it says it is. We stand firm on the inspired Word of God.

The Bible declares its inspiration: "All Scripture is inspired by God" (2 Timothy 3:16). The words *all Scripture* literally mean "every individual writing." Broadly applied, that's every word in the original

Hebrew, Aramaic, and Greek. And to the degree that our modern translations accurately render the original text, they, too, are authoritative. *All Scripture.* That means *all* parts are equally inspired. If you carry a red-letter edition of the Bible, the text in red isn't more inspired than the black print surrounding it. The red letters represent the words of Jesus, but they are no more inspired than the epistles of Paul, the writings of Moses, or the book of Revelation. The written Word of God comprises *all* Scripture. That includes the Old Testament, by the way. Just because you're a Christian doesn't mean that the gospel of Luke is more inspired than the book of Leviticus. You may have to work harder to glean the timeless truths from Leviticus, but they are just as relevant for you and me. Why? Because Leviticus—and *all* Scripture—is "inspired by God."

The word *inspired* comes from a unique term that appears only once in the New Testament. The Greek adjective *theopneustos* is a compound word from *theos*, meaning "God," and *pneustos*, meaning "spirit" or "breath."[1] The New International Version correctly renders the inimitable term: "All Scripture is *God-breathed*." That is its literal meaning.

The Scriptures are the God-breathed message from God to humankind. That means God superintended the human authors so that they used their individual personalities to compose and record Holy Scripture without error—right down to the very words themselves. This was not mindless dictation but the writing of various authors who were carried along in the process by the supernatural power of the Holy Spirit (2 Peter 1:21). The result? The Bible you have—yes, all sixty-six books—represents the very Word of God.

Let me define and explain three terms that are often confused:

- *Revelation* — God's *giving* of His truth
- *Inspiration* — Men's *writing* of God's truth
- *Illumination* — Our *being enlightened* by that same truth

The word *revelation* refers to God's giving of His Word to humankind — either in spoken or written form. That has ceased. There is no longer supernatural revelation given from God now that the Holy Scriptures are complete. After John wrote the last "Amen" in Revelation 22:21, we had all the revelation we needed for life and godliness found in the Bible (see 2 Peter 1:3–4). The word *inspiration* refers to the process of human writers recording, without error, the very words and mind of God. That's what "God-breathed" is all about! The work of inspiration has also ceased. The third term, *illumination*, refers to the understanding or insight the Holy Spirit gives one who reads or hears the written Word of God. Revelation has ceased. Inspiration has ceased. But illumination continues on; it occurs every day. It could even be occurring as you read the Scripture from this book.

Practically speaking, *illumination* plays the central role as you personally study and apply the Bible. Ask the Lord for guidance and for Him to illuminate His Word as you observe the text, interpret its literal meaning, and apply its truths. The Word of God is like a light that illumines our dark paths (Psalm 119:105; 2 Peter 1:19). It guides us. It provides direction. It gives us insight we would never have otherwise. Please join with me as we stand firm on the inspired Word of God.

# How to Begin a Relationship with God

Many have tried to plumb the depths of the Bible, to explore the cracks and crevices of its meaning. But for most of these adventurous souls, the Bible remains an enigma. These people would agree that it's a masterful collection of literature. They understand the words on the page, but something remains disconnected and elusive about the Bible. Whether these truth seekers know it or not, the question mark lodged in their minds was addressed by Paul in 1 Corinthians 2. He said God's wisdom is a mystery to those who do not have God's mind. Anyone can understand the surface truths of the Bible, but to understand the deeper truths one has to have the indwelling Spirit of God, who reveals the thoughts of God. The only way to have the Spirit of God dwelling within us is to believe in the Son of God. And to believe in the Son of God, we turn to the Word of God that reveals four essential truths we all must accept. Let's look at each one in detail.

## Our Spiritual Condition: Totally Depraved

The first truth is rather personal. One look in the mirror of Scripture, and our human condition becomes painfully clear:

"There is none righteous, not even one;
There is none who understands,
There is none who seeks for God;
All have turned aside, together they have become
    useless;
There is none who does good,
There is not even one." (Romans 3:10–12)

We are all sinners through and through—totally depraved. Now, that doesn't mean we've committed every atrocity known to humankind. We're not as *bad* as we can be, just as *bad off* as we can be. Sin colors all our thoughts, motives, words, and actions.

If you've been around a while, you likely already believe it. Look around. Everything around us bears the smudge marks of our sinful nature. Despite our best efforts to create a perfect world, crime statistics continue to soar, divorce rates keep climbing, and families keep crumbling.

Something has gone terribly wrong in our society and in ourselves—something deadly. Contrary to how the world would repackage it, "me-first" living doesn't equal rugged individuality and freedom; it equals death. As Paul said in his letter to the Romans, "The wages of sin is death" (Romans 6:23)—our spiritual and physical death that comes from God's righteous judgment of our sin, along with all of the emotional and practical effects of this separation that we experience on a daily basis. This brings us to the second marker: God's character.

## God's Character: Infinitely Holy

How can God judge us for a sinful state we were born into? Our total depravity is only half the answer. The other half is God's infinite holiness.

The fact that we know things are not as they should be points us to a standard of goodness beyond ourselves. Our sense of injustice in life on this side of eternity implies a perfect standard of justice beyond our reality. That standard and source is God Himself. And God's standard of holiness contrasts starkly with our sinful condition.

Scripture says that "God is Light, and in Him there is no darkness at all" (1 John 1:5). God is absolutely holy—which creates a problem for us. If He is so pure, how can we who are so impure relate to Him?

Perhaps we could try being better people, try to tilt the balance in favor of our good deeds, or seek out methods for self-improvement. Throughout history, people have attempted to live up to God's standard by keeping the Ten Commandments or living by their own code of ethics. Unfortunately, no one can come close to satisfying the demands of God's law. Romans 3:20 says, "By the works of the Law no flesh will be justified in His sight; for through the Law comes the knowledge of sin."

## Our Need: A Substitute

So here we are, sinners by nature and sinners by choice, trying to pull ourselves up by our own bootstraps to attain a relationship with our holy Creator. But every time we try, we fall flat on our faces. We can't live a good enough life to make up for our sin, because God's standard isn't "good enough"—it's *perfection*. And we can't make amends for the offense our sin has created without dying for it.

Who can get us out of this mess?

If someone could live perfectly, honoring God's law, and would bear sin's death penalty for us—in our place—then we would be saved from our predicament. But is there such a person? Thankfully, yes!

Meet your substitute—*Jesus Christ*. He is the One who took death's place for you!

> [God] made [Jesus Christ] who knew no sin to be sin on our behalf, so that we might become the righteousness of God in Him. (2 Corinthians 5:21)

## God's Provision: A Savior

God rescued us by sending His Son, Jesus, to die on the cross for our sins (1 John 4:9–10). Jesus was fully human and fully divine (John 1:1, 18), a truth that ensures His understanding of our weaknesses, His power to forgive, and His ability to bridge the gap between God and us (Romans 5:6–11). In short, we are "justified as a gift by His grace through the redemption which is in Christ Jesus" (Romans 3:24). Two words in this verse bear further explanation: *justified* and *redemption*.

*Justification* is God's act of mercy, in which He declares righteous the believing sinners while we are still in our sinning state. Justification doesn't mean that God *makes* us righteous, so that we never sin again, rather that He *declares* us righteous—much like a judge pardons a guilty criminal. Because Jesus took our sin upon Himself and suffered our judgment on the cross, God forgives our debt and proclaims us PARDONED.

*Redemption* is Christ's act of paying the complete price to release us from sin's bondage. God sent His Son to bear His wrath for all of our sins—past, present, and future (Romans 3:24–26; 2 Corinthians 5:21). In humble obedience, Christ willingly endured the shame of the cross for our sake (Mark 10:45; Romans 5:6–8; Philippians 2:8). Christ's death satisfied God's righteous demands. He no longer holds our sins against us, because His own Son paid the penalty for them. We are freed from the slave market of sin, never to be enslaved again!

## Placing Your Faith in Christ

These four truths describe how God has provided a way to Himself through Jesus Christ. Because the price has been paid in full by God, we must respond to His free gift of eternal life in total faith and confidence in Him to save us. We must step forward into the relationship with God that He has prepared for us—not by doing good works or by being a good person, but by coming to Him just as we are and accepting His justification and redemption by faith.

> For by grace you have been saved through faith;
> and that not of yourselves, it is the gift of God;
> not as a result of works, so that no one may boast.
> (Ephesians 2:8–9)

We accept God's gift of salvation simply by placing our faith in Christ alone for the forgiveness of our sins. Would you like to enter a relationship with your Creator by trusting in Christ as your Savior? If so, here's a simple prayer you can use to express your faith:

> *Dear God,*
>
> *I know that my sin has put a barrier between You and me. Thank You for sending Your Son, Jesus, to die in my place. I trust in Jesus alone to forgive my sins, and I accept His gift of eternal life. I ask Jesus to be my personal Savior and the Lord of my life. Thank You. In Jesus's name, amen.*

If you've prayed this prayer or one like it and you wish to find out more about knowing God and His plan for you in the Bible, contact us at Insight for Living Ministries. Our contact information is on the following pages.

# We Are Here for You

If you desire to find out more about knowing God and His plan for you in the Bible, contact us. Insight for Living Ministries provides staff pastors who are available for free written correspondence or phone consultation. These seminary-trained and seasoned counselors have years of experience and are well-qualified guides for your spiritual journey.

Please feel welcome to contact your regional office by using the information below:

**United States**
Insight for Living
Biblical Counseling Department
Post Office Box 269000
Plano, Texas 75026-9000
USA
972-473-5097 (Monday through Friday,
8:00 a.m.–5:00 p.m. central time)
www.insight.org/contactapastor

**Canada**
Insight for Living Canada
Biblical Counseling Department
PO Box 8 Stn A
Abbotsford BC V2T 6Z4
CANADA
1-800-663-7639
info@insightforliving.ca

**Australia, New Zealand, and South Pacific**
Insight for Living Australia
Pastoral Care
Post Office Box 443
Boronia, VIC 3155
AUSTRALIA
1300 467 444

**United Kingdom and Europe**
Insight for Living United Kingdom
Pastoral Care
PO Box 553
Dorking
RH4 9EU
UNITED KINGDOM
0800 787 9364
+44 (0)1306 640156
pastoralcare@insightforliving.org.uk

# Endnotes

## Orientation

1. Excerpted from Howard G. Hendricks and William D. Hendricks, *Living by the Book* (Chicago: Moody Press, 2007), 38–45. Used by permission.

## Step One: Observation

1. The fifteen books, in the order in which they appear in the paragraph: Mark, Luke, Kings, Acts, Revelation, James, Ruth, Numbers, Job, Amos, Esther, Judges, Titus, Lamentations, Hebrews.

2. G. K. Chesterton, "The Tremendous Adventures of Major Brown," in *Tell Me a Story: An Anthology*, ed. Charles Laughton (New York: McGraw-Hill, 1957), 140.

## Step Two: Interpretation

1. *The Point*, DVD, directed by Fred Wolf (1971; Burbank, Cal.: Fred Wolf Films, 2004).

2. C. S. Lewis, *Reflections on the Psalms* (New York: Harcourt, Brace, 1958), 3.

## Appendix: Inspiration

Adapted from Charles R. Swindoll, *The Church Awakening: An Urgent Call for Renewal* (New York: FaithWords, 2010), 190–195. Used by permission

1. Johannes P. Louw and Eugene A. Nida, eds., *Greek-English Lexicon of the New Testament Based on Semantic Domains*, 2nd ed. (New York: United Bible Societies, 1988, 1989). Electronic text hypertexted and prepared by OakTree Software, Inc. Version 3.2.

# Resources for Probing Further

No book in the world is like the Bible. In fact, the Bible is more than a book—it's a library of sixty-six volumes, covering a broad range of literary genres: history, biography, poetry, stories, proverbs, letters, and prophecy. But the Bible is so much more than that. Both great and small have discovered truth within its pages. Abraham Lincoln thought the Bible was God's greatest gift to humanity. And its impact on statesmen, artisans, and business people for millennia is unparalleled. So influential and masterful is the Bible, atheists have confessed that it's the world's greatest work of literary art and profound truth.

Yet the Bible is more than a masterpiece of literature and philosophy. Its greatness lies in the fact that it communicates the very mind and words of God. And for this reason the Bible transcends literature as it transforms lives. Every serious-minded person should make a serious study of this library of books. And the resources listed here are intended to help you do just that—to study and apply the truths of the Bible for yourself. Please keep in mind, however, as you peruse these resources that we can't always endorse everything a writer or ministry says, so we encourage you to approach these and all other non-biblical sources with wisdom and discernment.

Beitzel, Barry J. *The New Moody Atlas of the Bible*. Chicago: Moody, 2009.

Hendricks, Howard G., and William D. Hendricks. *Living by the Book*. Chicago: Moody Press, 2007.

Insight for Living. *Insight's Archaeology Handbook: Ten Key Finds and Why They Matter.* Plano, Tex.: IFL Publishing House, 2008.

Insight for Living. *Insight's Bible Handbook: Practical Helps for Bible Study.* Plano, Tex.: IFL Publishing House, 2007.

Insight for Living. *Insight's Handbook of New Testament Backgrounds: Key Customs from Each Book.* Plano, Tex.: IFL Publishing House, 2012.

Insight for Living. *Insight's New Testament Handbook: A Practical Look at Each Book.* Plano, Tex.: IFL Publishing House, 2010.

Insight for Living. *Insight's Old Testament Handbook: A Practical Look at Each Book.* Plano, Tex.: IFL Publishing House, 2009.

Packer, J. I., and M. C. Tenney, eds. *Illustrated Manners and Customs of the Bible.* Nashville: Thomas Nelson, 1997.

Swindoll, Charles R. *Saying It Well: Touching Others with Your Words.* New York: FaithWords, 2012.

Tenney, Merrill C., gen. ed. *The Zondervan Pictorial Encyclopedia of the Bible*, vols. 1–5. Grand Rapids: Regency Reference Library, 1976.

Tenney, Merrill C., gen. ed. *Zondervan's Pictorial Bible Dictionary.* Grand Rapids: Zondervan, 1967.

Traina, Robert A. *Methodical Bible Study.* Grand Rapids: Zondervan, 1985.

Virkler, Henry A., and Karelynne Gerber Ayayo. *Hermenutics: Principles and Processes of Biblical Interpretation*, 2nd. ed. Grand Rapids: Baker Academic, 2007.

Wald, Oletta. *The New Joy of Discovery in Bible Study.* Minneapolis: Augsburg Fortress, 2002.

Walvoord, John F. and Roy B. Zuck, eds. *The Bible Knowledge Commentary: New Testament.* Wheaton, Ill.: Victor Books, 1983.

Walvoord, John F. and Roy B. Zuck, eds. *The Bible Knowledge Commentary: Old Testament.* Wheaton, Ill.: Victor Books, 1986.

Zuck, Roy B. *Basic Bible Interpretation: A Practical Guide to Discovering Biblical Truth.* Colorado Springs: Chariot Victor, 1991.

# Ordering Information

If you would like to order additional copies of *Taking Aim: How to Accurately Apply Scripture* or order other Insight for Living Ministries resources, please contact the office that serves you.

**United States**
Insight for Living
Post Office Box 269000
Plano, Texas 75026-9000
USA
1-800-772-8888
(Monday through Friday,
7:00 a.m.–7:00 p.m. central time)
www.insight.org
www.insightworld.org

**Canada**
Insight for Living Canada
PO Box 8 Stn A
Abbotsford BC V2T 6Z4
CANADA
1-800-663-7639
www.insightforliving.ca

**Australia, New Zealand, and South Pacific**
Insight for Living Australia
Post Office Box 443
Boronia, VIC 3155
AUSTRALIA
1300 467 444
www.insight.asn.au

**United Kingdom and Europe**
Insight for Living United Kingdom
PO Box 553
Dorking
RH4 9EU
UNITED KINGDOM
0800 787 9364
www.insightforliving.org.uk

**Other International Locations**
International constituents may contact the U.S. office through our Web site (www.insightworld.org), mail queries, or by calling +1-972-473-5136.